CONTENTS

THE ULTIMATE SUMMER SOCIAL MEDIA PLAYBOOK:

*Boost Your Business in the
Heat of the Season*

Empower Your Business

www.vitalixdigital.ca

Schedule your Free Strategy Session Now

Learn more about our Social Media Packages

INTRODUCTION:

I magine a small ice cream shop struggling to attract customers during the hot summer months. Despite offering delicious treats, they find it challenging to stand out amidst stiff competition and a crowded market.

However, they decide to take advantage of summer social media trends and themes to revamp their marketing strategy. They start by creating eye-catching posts featuring their mouthwatering ice cream cones against vibrant summer backgrounds. They incorporate popular summer hashtags like #SummerTreats and #CoolDownWithIceCream to increase visibility.

To engage their audience further, they run a summer-themed contest encouraging followers to share their favorite ice cream memories for a chance to win free treats. This not only generates excitement but also encourages user-generated content, expanding their reach organically.

Additionally, they offer exclusive "Heatwave Deals" through their social media channels, promoting limited-time discounts and special offers to attract new customers and reward loyal ones.

As a result of their strategic approach to summer social media marketing, the ice cream shop experiences a surge in foot traffic and online orders. They see a significant increase in engagement on their social media platforms, with followers eagerly sharing their posts and spreading the word about their delicious summer treats.

By leveraging the power of social media and tapping into the spirit of summer, the ice cream shop not only survives but thrives during the hottest months of the year, establishing itself as a go-to destination for summer indulgence in the community.

Here's how you can do that too…

CHAPTER 1: CRAFTING SUMMER-THEMED CONTENT

Welcome to The Ultimate Summer Social Media Playbook! In this guide, we'll explore how you can make the most out of the scorching summer months to elevate your social media presence and drive business growth. From crafting compelling content to leveraging trending topics, we've got you covered with actionable strategies and tips to captivate your audience and stand out in the crowded digital landscape. Let's dive in and transform your summer strategy!

Understanding The Summer Mindset

As the temperature rises and the days stretch longer, it's time to tap into the summer spirit and make waves with your marketing. But first, let's talk about the summer mindset and how it can influence your business strategies. Summer isn't just a season; it's a state of mind. It's all about warmth, relaxation, and the great outdoors. But what does this mean for your business? Well, buckle up, because we're about to dive into how understanding the summer mindset can supercharge your marketing efforts.

Picture this: as the sun shines brighter, so do people's moods. They're itching to get out there, explore, and indulge in some well-deserved fun. From impromptu road trips to backyard BBQs, summer is the time when consumers are more open to spending on leisure activities and treats.

And let's not forget about the online world. With longer days and warmer nights, social media platforms are buzzing with summer vibes. People are sharing their adventures, seeking inspiration, and connecting with brands that embrace the laid-back, adventurous spirit of the season.

So, how can you leverage this summer frenzy to boost your business? It's simple, really. By crafting content that resonates with the summer mindset, you'll capture the attention of your audience and stand out in the crowd. Think vibrant imagery, seasonal themes, and storytelling that transports them to those carefree summer days.

Understanding the summer season isn't just about riding the wave of sunshine—it's about connecting with your audience on a deeper level and creating content that speaks to their summer-loving souls. So, grab your sunglasses and get ready to shine bright this summer with your marketing efforts!

Examples:

- **Ice Cream Shop:** Create content that evokes the joy of summer treats, such as colorful ice cream cones against a backdrop of sunny beaches or picnics in the park.
- **Realtor:** Share tips for staging homes for summer open houses, highlighting features like backyard patios and swimming pools to appeal to summer

homebuyers.

- **Plumber:** Offer advice on summer plumbing maintenance, such as preparing outdoor faucets for irrigation systems and checking for leaks in sprinkler systems.
- **Medi Spa:** Showcase summer skincare tips, focusing on protecting skin from sun damage and staying hydrated in the heat with refreshing facial mists and hydrating masks.
- **Nutritionist/Coach:** Share seasonal recipes featuring fresh, summer produce like berries, cucumbers, and tomatoes, along with tips for staying hydrated and nourished during outdoor activities.

Tapping Into Summer Experiences

As a business owner, understanding and tapping into the essence of summer experiences can significantly elevate your marketing game. It's not just about selling products or services; it's about connecting with your audience on a personal level and becoming a part of their summer memories. Let's explore how you can do just that.

Summer is a time of adventure and exploration, with people eagerly planning vacations, attending festivals, and soaking up the sun on beach days. By keeping your finger on the pulse of trending summer activities, you can tailor your content to align with what your audience is already excited about. Whether it's creating vacation-inspired promotions, sharing tips for navigating festivals, or curating beach day essentials, tapping into these trends shows that you're in tune with your audience's interests and passions.

One of the most effective ways to connect with your audience is by sharing authentic, real-life summer experiences. Whether it's a behind-the-scenes look at your team's summer retreat, a glimpse into how your products enhance outdoor adventures, or a showcase of customers enjoying your services at a summer event, incorporating these experiences into your content adds a personal touch that resonates with your audience. It's not just about selling; it's about inviting your audience to be a part of your summer journey.

User-generated content (UGC) is a powerful tool for showcasing the summer fun that your brand facilitates. Encourage your customers to share their summer experiences with your products or services on social media, and then leverage that content to amplify your brand's presence. Whether it's reposting customer photos enjoying your products at the beach, sharing testimonials from satisfied festival attendees, or featuring user-generated videos of people using your services at backyard barbecues, UGC adds authenticity and credibility to your brand while also showcasing the diverse ways that people incorporate your offerings into their summer adventures.

By tapping into trending summer activities, incorporating real-life experiences into your content, and leveraging user-generated content, you can create a summer marketing strategy that not only resonates with your audience but also positions your brand as an essential part of their summer experiences. So, embrace the summer vibes, get creative with your content, and let your audience know that you're ready to make this summer unforgettable together!

Examples:

- **Ice Cream Shop:** Host a "Sundae Funday" event where customers can create their own customized ice cream sundaes with a variety of toppings and flavors.
- **Realtor:** Organize neighborhood ice cream socials as a fun way to bring together potential homebuyers and showcase properties in the community.
- **Plumber:** Offer summer promotions on services like outdoor faucet repair and sprinkler system installation to help homeowners prepare for the season.
- **Medi Spa:** Launch a "Summer Glow" campaign featuring specials on rejuvenating treatments like hydrating facials and body scrubs to get clients ready for summer.
- **Nutritionist/Coach:** Host a series of outdoor cooking classes focused on healthy summer eating, featuring recipes for grilling vegetables and making refreshing smoothies.

Showcasing Your Brand's Summer Story

Summer isn't just about soaking up the sun; it's also a prime opportunity to showcase your brand's personality, values, and unique story. By infusing your summer-themed content with your brand's essence, you can create meaningful connections with your audience and stand out in the crowded digital landscape. Let's dive into how you can authentically communicate your brand message this summer.

Every brand has a story to tell, and summer provides the perfect backdrop for sharing yours. Whether it's the journey of how your business came to be, the inspiration behind your products or services, or the values that drive your company forward, crafting and sharing your brand's unique summer narrative adds depth and authenticity to your content. Consider incorporating elements of nostalgia, adventure, or community into your storytelling to resonate with your audience on a deeper level.

Summer presents a golden opportunity to showcase your brand's summer-specific products or services. Whether it's refreshing beverages, outdoor gear, or seasonal experiences, highlighting these offerings in your content allows you to tap into the season's excitement and meet your audience's summer needs. From featuring your latest summer collection to sharing tips on how to make the most of your products during the sunny season, let your audience know that you're here to enhance their summer experience.

Summer-themed campaigns offer a creative way to tell your brand's story and connect with your audience. Whether it's a summer sale, a themed giveaway, or a charity initiative tied to summer activities, crafting campaigns that align with the season allows you to engage your audience in a meaningful way while also driving business objectives. Consider incorporating summer-themed visuals, hashtags, and messaging to create a cohesive and impactful campaign that resonates with your audience's summer spirit.

When it comes to storytelling, the key is to engage your audience's emotions and leave a lasting impression. Whether you're sharing customer testimonials, behind-the-scenes glimpses of your team's summer adventures, or heartfelt anecdotes that showcase your brand's values, employing engaging storytelling techniques adds depth and authenticity to your content. Consider incorporating multimedia elements such as videos, photos, and interactive features to captivate your audience and make your brand's summer story truly memorable.

Examples:

- **Ice Cream Shop:** Share behind-the-scenes stories of how your artisanal ice cream is made, highlighting locally sourced ingredients and seasonal flavors.
- **Realtor:** Create video testimonials from happy clients who found their dream homes during the summer months, emphasizing the positive experiences of buying or selling during this season.
- **Plumber:** Showcase before-and-after photos of outdoor plumbing projects, such as installing outdoor showers or repairing poolside plumbing fixtures, to demonstrate your expertise in summer plumbing solutions.
- **Medi Spa:** Feature client success stories and transformations achieved through your summer skincare treatments, highlighting the confidence and radiance they gained.
- **Nutritionist/Coach:** Share testimonials from clients who achieved their health and fitness goals with your guidance, showcasing their summer

transformations and improved well-being.

Failing to incorporate summer-themed content into your marketing strategy could result in missed opportunities to effectively engage with your audience during a season when they are most active and receptive to relevant content. For instance, imagine an ice cream shop neglecting to highlight their summer flavors and promotions on social media. This oversight could lead to lost sales and decreased customer interactions, especially during the peak ice cream season.

Moreover, failing to align your content with the summer season may cause your brand to be perceived as out-of-touch or irrelevant to current trends and interests. Consider a scenario where a realtor continues to share generic property listings without emphasizing summer-specific features. As a result, potential buyers may overlook these listings in favor of competitors who showcase homes tailored to the season, ultimately leading to decreased engagement and interest from the audience.

Additionally, neglecting to tap into the emotions and experiences associated with summer could hinder your ability to establish a strong emotional connection with your audience. For example, a nutritionist who fails to share summer-specific wellness tips and recipes may struggle to keep followers engaged, as they seek content that resonates with their seasonal lifestyle and goals.

On the other hand, by crafting summer-themed content, you can enhance engagement levels with your audience as they relate to the seasonal themes and experiences. Picture an ice cream shop creating vibrant and playful social media posts featuring their summer flavors. This approach could result in increased likes, comments, and shares from followers eager to explore the latest offerings.

Furthermore, aligning your content with the summer season can bolster your brand image and perception as relevant, timely, and in tune with current trends. Consider a realtor who shares captivating photos of summer homes with inviting outdoor spaces. Such content positions them as experts catering to clients' desires for seasonal living and leisure.

Lastly, summer-themed content offers a unique opportunity to connect with your audience on a personal level by tapping into shared experiences and emotions associated with the season. For instance, imagine a nutritionist sharing refreshing summer smoothie recipes and wellness tips. This content fosters a sense of camaraderie and support among followers striving to maintain healthy habits during the warmer months.

CHAPTER 2: LEVERAGING TRENDING TOPICS AND HOLIDAYS

Staying Ahead of the Curve

Stay informed about the latest trends and conversations happening in your industry and community. By monitoring trending topics, you can position your brand as a relevant and timely voice in the social media landscape.

Examples:

- **Ice Cream Shop:** Stay on top of trending flavor combinations and create limited-time offerings inspired by popular summer trends, such as tropical fruit flavors or nostalgic childhood favorites.
- **Realtor:** Share timely market updates and insights related to summer real estate trends, such as rising demand for homes with outdoor living spaces or waterfront properties.
- **Plumber:** Offer tips and advice on social media for preventing common summer plumbing issues, such as clogged drains from outdoor entertaining or sewer line backups due to heavy rainfall.

- **Medi Spa:** Capitalize on summer beauty trends by offering seasonal treatments like sun-kissed spray tans or beach-ready waxing services, and promoting them through targeted social media campaigns.
- **Nutritionist/Coach:** Address popular summer wellness topics like staying fit while traveling or navigating social gatherings with healthy eating tips and strategies to keep clients on track with their goals.

In today's dynamic digital landscape, staying ahead of the curve is crucial for maintaining relevance and visibility. To achieve this, it's essential to keep a close eye on the latest trends and conversations happening in your industry and community. By monitoring social media trends and conversations, you can gain valuable insights into what topics are resonating with your audience and how their interests may be evolving over the summer months.

Moreover, it's important to adapt quickly to emerging summer trends. As the season progresses, new themes, interests, and activities may emerge that capture the attention of your audience. By staying nimble and responsive, you can ensure that your content remains timely and relevant, positioning your brand as a trusted source of information and inspiration during the sunny season.

Here are some examples of emerging summer trends that have influenced business marketing strategies in the past:

1. **Outdoor Fitness Boom:** With the rise of outdoor fitness activities such as hiking, biking, and

outdoor yoga, businesses in the health and wellness industry have adapted their marketing strategies to promote outdoor-friendly products and services. This trend has led to the creation of summer-themed workout programs, outdoor fitness events, and partnerships with outdoor gear brands.

2. **Sustainable Summer:** As consumers become more conscious of their environmental footprint, businesses across various industries have shifted towards offering eco-friendly products and services. This trend has influenced marketing strategies to highlight sustainability efforts, promote green initiatives, and educate consumers on eco-friendly practices for summer activities such as camping, picnicking, and outdoor events.

3. **Staycation Culture:** The rise of staycation culture, particularly during times of travel restrictions or economic downturns, has led businesses in the hospitality and tourism industry to adapt their marketing strategies to cater to local travelers. This trend has resulted in the promotion of staycation packages, local experiences, and destination marketing campaigns aimed at encouraging residents to explore their own backyard.

4. **Virtual Events and Experiences:** With the advent of technology and the widespread use of social media, businesses have increasingly turned to virtual events and experiences to engage with their audience during the summer months. This trend has led to the creation of virtual concerts,

online festivals, and digital workshops, allowing businesses to reach a wider audience and adapt to changing consumer preferences for remote entertainment and engagement.

5. **Wellness Retreats and Self-Care:** The growing interest in wellness and self-care has influenced businesses to offer summer-themed wellness retreats, spa packages, and self-care products aimed at promoting relaxation and rejuvenation during the summer months. This trend has led to the creation of marketing campaigns centered around mindfulness, stress relief, and holistic health practices, catering to consumers seeking a break from the hustle and bustle of everyday life.

To facilitate trend analysis and stay ahead of the curve, consider utilizing a variety of tools and strategies. Social media listening tools can help you track mentions, hashtags, and conversations related to summer topics, allowing you to identify emerging trends and topics of interest to your audience. Additionally, pay attention to data analytics and insights provided by social media platforms, which can offer valuable information about audience demographics, engagement patterns, and content performance. By keeping your finger on the pulse of what's happening in your industry and community, you can ensure that your content remains fresh, engaging, and aligned with the evolving interests and preferences of your audience.

Harnessing The Power Of Summer Holidays

Summer is filled with holidays and events that present opportunities for creative marketing campaigns. From Canada Day to National Ice Cream Day, explore how to incorporate summer holidays into your content calendar to drive engagement and connect with your audience.

Examples:

- **Ice Cream Shop:** Run promotions and special events tied to summer holidays like National Ice Cream Day, offering discounts, giveaways, and themed treats to celebrate with customers.
- **Realtor:** Create themed social media content around local events whether it's a parade, a holiday like Canada Day or just a summer shindig. Highlighting homes with patriotic decor or hosting virtual tours of properties with outdoor entertaining spaces for summer celebrations.
- **Plumber:** Share tips for preventing plumbing emergencies during holiday weekends, such as advising homeowners to avoid disposing of grease down drains or to be mindful of overusing garbage disposals during outdoor barbeques.
- **Medi Spa:** Offer holiday-themed spa packages and treatments, such as a "Red, White, and Beautiful" facial package for Canada Day or a "Labor Day Relaxation Retreat" featuring massages and aromatherapy.
- **Nutritionist/Coach:** Create holiday-inspired meal plans and recipes for clients to enjoy during summer celebrations, focusing on healthy alternatives to traditional barbecue fare or refreshing mocktail recipes for outdoor gatherings.

Without leveraging trending topics and holidays in your marketing efforts, it could result in missed opportunities to stay relevant and engage with your audience during peak periods of interest and activity. For example, imagine a clothing retailer failing to capitalize on the buzz surrounding summer fashion trends. This oversight could lead to decreased engagement and sales as competitors effectively leverage trending topics to capture consumer attention.

Furthermore, failing to harness the power of summer holidays may cause your brand to appear disconnected from the cultural zeitgeist, leading to decreased interest and engagement from your audience. Consider a scenario where a restaurant neglects to promote special menu offerings for Canada Day celebrations. This oversight could result in missed opportunities to attract diners looking to commemorate the holiday with themed dining experiences, ultimately impacting the restaurant's bottom line.

On the other hand, by actively incorporating trending topics and holidays into your marketing strategy, you can position your brand as current, relatable, and in tune with the interests of your audience. Picture a coffee shop creating social media posts featuring summer-inspired beverages and promotions in anticipation of National Iced Coffee Day. This approach could generate excitement and engagement among followers eager to celebrate the occasion with their favorite caffeinated treats.

Moreover, leveraging trending topics and holidays provides an opportunity to tap into the collective enthusiasm and sentiment surrounding these events, fostering a sense of community and connection with your audience. For instance, imagine a tech company launching a social media campaign centered around the excitement of the summer solstice. By encouraging followers to share their favorite summer tech gadgets and experiences, the company can cultivate a sense of camaraderie and engagement within its online community.

In summary, integrating trending topics and holidays into your marketing strategy is essential for maintaining relevance, driving engagement, and fostering a sense of connection with your audience. By staying attuned to the cultural landscape and leveraging these opportunities strategically, you can elevate your brand's visibility and appeal during the summer season and beyond.

CHAPTER 3: IMPLEMENTING EFFECTIVE HASHTAG STRATEGIES

Mastering Hashtag Research

Hashtags are a powerful tool for increasing the visibility of your content and reaching new audiences. Learn how to conduct hashtag research to identify relevant and trending hashtags that resonate with your target audience.

Examples:

- **Ice Cream Shop:** Research popular summer-related hashtags like #SummerTreats or #CoolDownWithIceCream and incorporate them into your posts to increase visibility and reach a wider audience of summer enthusiasts.
- **Realtor:** Use local hashtags specific to your market area along with broader real estate-related hashtags like #DreamHome or #HouseHunting to

attract potential buyers and sellers during the summer season.

- **Plumber:** Utilize industry-specific hashtags like #PlumbingTips or #SummerPlumbing along with location-based hashtags to connect with homeowners in need of summer plumbing services in your area.
- **Medi Spa:** Incorporate trending beauty and wellness hashtags like #SummerSkincare or #GlowingSkin into your posts to engage with a community of skincare enthusiasts seeking summer beauty tips and treatments.
- **Nutritionist/Coach:** Explore hashtags related to healthy living and wellness such as #HealthySummerEating or #FitFam to share your summer nutrition tips and connect with clients interested in improving their well-being during the summer months.

Developing Branded Hashtags:

Create and promote branded hashtags to foster community engagement and brand advocacy. Discover how to encourage your audience to use your branded hashtags and become ambassadors for your brand on social media.

Examples:

- **Ice Cream Shop:** Create a branded hashtag like #ScoopOfSummer or #ChillWith[ShopName] and encourage customers to use it when sharing photos of their favorite ice cream treats for a chance to be featured on your social media accounts.

- **Realtor:** Establish a branded hashtag such as #[AgencyName]Homes or #[NeighborhoodName]Dreams and encourage clients to use it when sharing photos and testimonials of their home buying or selling experiences with your agency.
- **Plumber:** Launch a branded hashtag like #[CompanyName]PlumbingPros or #[CityName]PlumbingSolutions and promote it on social media to encourage customers to share their positive experiences and recommendations for your plumbing services.
- **Medi Spa:** Introduce a branded hashtag such as #[ClinicName]GlowGoals or #[BeautyTreatment]Babes and use it to showcase client transformations and share before-and-after photos of your summer skincare treatments.
- **Nutritionist/Coach:** Start a branded hashtag like #[YourName]HealthySummer or #[NutritionPractice]WellnessJourney and invite clients to use it when sharing their summer fitness and nutrition successes to inspire others and build a supportive online community.

Implementation of effective hashtag strategies in your social media marketing efforts is critical as without them it can lead to missed opportunities to expand your reach and decreased visibility across platforms. Some may argue that hashtags are useless, but this is only true if you don't use them the right way. For instance, envision a small boutique neglecting to use relevant summer-themed hashtags in their Instagram posts. This oversight could result in limited exposure to potential customers who are actively searching for summer fashion inspiration and trends.

Additionally, overlooking the development of branded hashtags specific to your business may hinder your ability to cultivate a cohesive brand identity and encourage user-generated content. Consider a scenario where a fitness studio fails to establish a unique branded hashtag for their community of members to use when sharing workout photos and success stories. Without a designated hashtag, the studio misses out on the opportunity to foster a sense of belonging and community among its followers.

On the contrary, by implementing effective hashtag strategies, you can amplify your social media presence and enhance discoverability among relevant audiences. Imagine a travel agency incorporating popular summer travel hashtags like #SummerGetaway and #ExploreYourWorld into their posts. This strategic use of hashtags increases the likelihood of their content being seen by individuals actively seeking travel inspiration and tips for summer vacations.

Furthermore, developing branded hashtags allows you to create a unified experience for your audience and facilitate engagement with your brand. Picture a wellness brand introducing a branded hashtag like #HealthySummerLiving for their community to share their wellness journeys and experiences. This hashtag not only encourages user-generated content but also strengthens brand loyalty and recognition as followers actively participate in the conversation. By strategically incorporating relevant hashtags and developing branded hashtags, you can optimize your social media presence and establish a meaningful connection with your audience during the summer season and beyond.

CHAPTER 4: ANALYZING SUMMER ANALYTICS AND METRICS

Setting Summer-Specific Goals

Define key performance indicators (KPIs) tailored to your summer social media objectives. Whether it's increasing engagement or driving website traffic, establish clear goals to measure the success of your summer strategy.

Example:

- **Ice Cream Shop:** Set goals to increase summer foot traffic by a certain percentage compared to the previous year, track the number of social media mentions during peak summer months, and aim to boost online orders for summer-themed ice cream cakes and party packs.
- **Realtor:** Establish objectives to generate a higher number of leads through summer open houses

and virtual tours, track website traffic and engagement from summer-specific content, and aim to secure a certain percentage of listings or sales during the summer season.

- **Plumber:** Define targets to increase summer service calls for outdoor plumbing repairs and installations, monitor customer satisfaction ratings and reviews during peak summer months, and aim to expand your summer client base through targeted marketing efforts.
- **Medi Spa:** Set benchmarks to increase summer bookings for popular treatments like laser hair removal and chemical peels, track the number of inquiries and consultations received through summer promotions, and aim to boost revenue from summer skincare product sales.
- **Nutritionist/Coach:** Establish goals to grow your summer client roster through targeted marketing campaigns and referrals, track client progress and satisfaction with summer wellness programs and challenges, and aim to increase engagement and followers on social media with summer-themed content.

Interpreting Summer Analytics

Dive into the data to gain insights into your audience's preferences, behaviors, and engagement patterns. By analyzing summer analytics and metrics, you can refine your strategy and make informed decisions to optimize your social media performance.

Examples:

- **Ice Cream Shop:** Analyze summer analytics to identify peak days and times for foot traffic and online orders, track which summer flavors and promotions generated the most buzz and sales, and use customer feedback and reviews to refine your summer menu offerings and marketing strategies.
- **Realtor:** Dive into summer analytics to uncover trends in property searches and inquiries, identify which summer marketing campaigns and listings attracted the most attention and leads, and leverage data insights to optimize your summer advertising budget and targeting strategies.
- **Plumber:** Interpret summer analytics to pinpoint common plumbing issues and service requests during the season, track customer satisfaction and referrals from summer clients, and use data-driven insights to improve your summer service offerings and customer experience.
- **Medi Spa:** Review summer analytics to assess the effectiveness of your summer promotions and campaigns, identify popular treatments and services among summer clients, and leverage data insights to tailor your summer marketing efforts and service offerings to meet client demand.
- **Nutritionist/Coach:** Analyze summer analytics to understand client engagement and progress with summer wellness programs and challenges, track the performance of summer content and campaigns on social media, and use data insights to refine your summer coaching and content strategies to better serve your audience.

Remember to analyze summer analytics and metrics to

better understand your audience's behavior and optimize your social media strategy for maximum impact. It's important to remember that while analytics provide valuable insights, it's equally important not to get discouraged too quickly. Some strategies take time and patience to yield results, and analytics can help us understand what's working and what needs adjustment.

Moreover, it's easy to get caught up in the underperformance of certain key performance indicators (KPIs), but it's essential to use these as future learning opportunities rather than sources of discouragement. For instance, envision an e-commerce store becoming disheartened by low conversion rates on their summer promotion posts. Instead of giving up on the strategy altogether, they can use analytics to identify areas for improvement, such as refining their targeting or adjusting their messaging to better resonate with their audience.

On the contrary, by diligently analyzing summer analytics and metrics, you can gain valuable insights into the effectiveness of your social media efforts and make data-driven decisions to optimize your strategy. Imagine a fashion brand reviewing their summer analytics to identify which posts generated the highest engagement and conversion rates. Armed with this information, they can replicate successful strategies and tailor future content to better meet their audience's preferences and interests.

Furthermore, analytics provide an opportunity to measure the impact of your social media efforts on overarching business goals, such as increased brand awareness, website traffic, and sales. Picture a technology company tracking the correlation between their summer social media campaigns and website traffic. By analyzing referral sources and user behavior, they can assess the effectiveness of their social media strategy in driving valuable traffic to their website and converting leads into customers.

By embracing analytics as valuable tools for learning and improvement, you can gain actionable insights into your audience's behavior, identify areas for optimization, and make informed decisions to drive success during the summer season and beyond.

CHAPTER 5: CREATING COMPELLING VISUALS AND GRAPHICS

Capturing Attention With Visuals

Visual content is essential for grabbing the attention of your audience on social media. Explore design principles and tools for creating stunning graphics and images that command attention and evoke emotion.

Examples:

- **Ice Cream Shop:** Create mouthwatering visuals of your summer ice cream creations, such as vibrant scoops piled high on waffle cones or elaborate sundae creations topped with fresh fruit and colorful sprinkles.
- **Realtor:** Showcase stunning images of summer homes and outdoor spaces, including lush gardens, inviting pools, and panoramic views

of beaches or mountains, to captivate potential buyers and inspire their dream home visions.

- **Plumber:** Share before-and-after photos of outdoor plumbing projects and repairs, such as installing outdoor showers or revamping backyard irrigation systems, to demonstrate your expertise and the transformative power of your services.
- **Medi Spa:** Feature captivating visuals of your summer skincare treatments and services, including serene spa settings, luxurious treatment rooms, and satisfied clients enjoying rejuvenating facials and body treatments.
- **Nutritionist/Coach:** Share vibrant images of summer-inspired healthy meals and snacks, such as colorful salads, refreshing smoothies, and grilled fruit skewers, to inspire your audience to embrace nutritious eating habits during the summer months.

Embracing Video Content

Video marketing is a powerful way to tell your brand's story and engage your audience. Learn how to create engaging video content that captivates your audience and drives meaningful interactions on social media.

Examples:

- **Ice Cream Shop:** Create fun and engaging video content of behind-the-scenes footage showing how your summer ice cream flavors are made, from churning creamy bases to adding swirls of seasonal fruit and crunchy toppings.

- **Realtor:** Produce virtual tours and video walkthroughs of summer properties, highlighting key features like outdoor entertaining areas, scenic views, and nearby attractions to give potential buyers a taste of the summer lifestyle.
- **Plumber:** Share informative how-to videos and tutorials on summer plumbing maintenance tips and DIY repairs, demonstrating tasks like cleaning gutters, inspecting outdoor faucets, and unclogging drains to help homeowners prepare for the season.
- **Medi Spa:** Showcase video testimonials and client testimonials sharing their summer skincare journeys and experiences with your spa, featuring before-and-after shots and heartfelt testimonials to inspire confidence in your services.
- Nutritionist/Coach: Create cooking demonstration videos and recipe tutorials featuring summer-inspired dishes and healthy eating tips, guiding your audience through the preparation of seasonal meals and snacks to support their wellness goals during the summer months.

Overlooking the creation of compelling visuals and graphics for your social media content can limit your ability to capture audience attention and stand out in crowded feeds. However, it's important to address common concerns, such as feeling self-conscious about being on camera, and to explore alternative solutions, like reaching out to local photographers and videographers for assistance.

Moreover, it's understandable that not everyone feels comfortable being on camera, but it's essential to overcome these obstacles to effectively engage with your audience. To address concerns about appearance and voice, consider practicing self-compassion and focusing on delivering valuable content rather than worrying about perfection. Remember, authenticity resonates with audiences, and imperfections can humanize your brand and make you more relatable.

Additionally, consider reaching out to local photographers and videographers who can help bring your vision to life and create professional-quality content for your social media channels. Collaborating with professionals can elevate the visual appeal of your content and provide fresh perspectives and creative ideas to enhance your brand image.

Furthermore, if hiring professionals isn't feasible, there are still ways to create high-quality videos yourself. Start by investing in a good quality camera or smartphone with decent video capabilities. Experiment with different angles, lighting, and backgrounds to find what works best for your brand aesthetic. Additionally, consider using editing tools and apps to enhance the visual appeal of your videos and add professional touches.

Tips And Tricks For Product Photography

- **Food Photography:** Experiment with different angles to showcase the textures and colors of your dishes. Try shooting from above (flat lay), at a 45-degree angle, or even from a low angle to add depth and visual interest. Pay attention to lighting, as natural light can enhance the vibrancy of your food photos.

- **Clothing Photography:** When photographing clothing items, consider using a mannequin or model to showcase how the garment fits and drapes. Experiment with different poses and angles to highlight key features and details, such as fabric texture, patterns, and embellishments. Utilize natural light or soft, diffused artificial light to minimize harsh shadows and ensure accurate color representation.

Additional Tips For Taking Good Photos

- **Composition:** Pay attention to composition techniques such as the rule of thirds, leading lines, and framing to create visually appealing photos. Experiment with different compositions to find the most effective way to convey your message and capture the viewer's attention.
- **Background and Props:** Choose backgrounds and props that compliment your products and enhance their visual appeal. Consider using props such as flowers, foliage, or decorative elements to add context and interest to your photos without overshadowing the main subject.
- **Editing:** Use photo editing tools and apps

to enhance your photos and correct any imperfections. Adjust factors such as brightness, contrast, saturation, and sharpness to achieve the desired look and feel. However, be mindful not to over-edit your photos, as this can detract from their authenticity and realism.

Ultimately, by addressing common concerns about being on camera and exploring alternative solutions, such as collaborating with local photographers and videographers and applying some of the photography tips and tricks, you can elevate the visual appeal of your content and engage with your audience in meaningful ways during the summer season and beyond.

CHAPTER 6: ENGAGING WITH FOLLOWERS THROUGH CONTESTS AND CHALLENGES

Spark Excitement With Contests

Interactive contests are a fun and effective way to engage your audience and drive user-generated content. Explore different types of social media contests and learn how to design and execute engaging contests that inspire participation and foster community.

Examples:

- **Ice Cream Shop:** Host a "Create Your Own Flavor"

contest where followers can submit their ideas for a new summer ice cream flavor, with the winning flavor being featured as a limited-time offering on your menu.

- **Realtor:** Launch a "Summer Dream Home Giveaway" contest where participants can enter to win a weekend getaway or summer-themed prize pack by sharing their dream home wish list or favorite summer home feature on social media.
- **Plumber:** Run a "Summer Plumbing Makeover" contest where homeowners can submit photos of their outdoor plumbing projects or summer plumbing challenges for a chance to win a free plumbing inspection or service call.
- **Medi Spa:** Host a "Summer Glow Challenge" where participants can share their skincare routines and transformations over the summer months, with weekly prizes awarded for the most radiant skin and inspiring testimonials.
- **Nutritionist/Coach:** Create a "Summer Wellness Challenge" where participants can commit to healthy habits and self-care practices throughout the summer, with daily challenges and accountability check-ins to support their goals

Foster Community With Challenges

Challenges are a great way to foster camaraderie and strengthen brand loyalty among your audience. Discover how to create challenges that inspire creativity, encourage collaboration, and build a sense of belonging within your community.

Examples:

- **Ice Cream Shop:** Encourage customers to participate in a "Sundae Sunday Challenge" where they can share photos of their most creative ice cream sundaes and vote for their favorites, fostering a sense of community and friendly competition among ice cream lovers.
- **Realtor:** Organize a "Summer Scavenger Hunt" challenge where participants can explore local neighborhoods and landmarks, sharing photos and clues along the way to uncover hidden gems and win prizes.
- **Plumber:** Launch a "Summer Home Maintenance Challenge" where homeowners can share their DIY projects and home improvement tips, fostering a supportive community of homeowners sharing resources and expertise.
- **Medi Spa:** Create a "Summer Self-Care Challenge" where participants can commit to prioritizing self-care and wellness activities throughout the summer, sharing their experiences and encouraging others to join in the journey.
- **Nutritionist/Coach:** Host a "Summer Fitness Challenge" where participants can set fitness goals and track their progress over the summer months, sharing workout routines, healthy recipes, and motivational tips to inspire others in the community.

Neglecting to engage with followers through interactive contests and challenges may hinder your ability to grow your social media following and cultivate a thriving community around your brand. However, it's important to address the big question of *"how do I get more followers?"* in order to even create a community.

Growing your social media following requires a strategic approach and consistent effort. For example, a local coffee shop looking to attract more followers might partner with a nearby bookstore for a "Bookworms' Brew" giveaway, where participants can win a coffee gift basket and a selection of best-selling books. By cross-promoting the giveaway on both the coffee shop's and the bookstore's social media channels, they can reach new audiences interested in coffee and literature.

Additionally, engaging with your existing followers through interactive polls, quizzes, and behind-the-scenes content can help foster loyalty and attract new followers who resonate with your brand's personality and values. For instance, a sustainable fashion brand could host a weekly "Eco-Friendly Fashion Challenge," encouraging followers to share photos of their thrifted or upcycled outfits for a chance to be featured on the brand's social media accounts. This interactive challenge not only showcases the brand's commitment to sustainability but also encourages community participation and engagement.

Furthermore, consider leveraging user-generated content and encouraging followers to share their experiences with your brand. For example, a pet grooming salon could create a dedicated hashtag like #PamperedPawsMonday and invite customers to share photos of their freshly groomed pets every Monday. By reposting these photos on their own social media channels and offering discounts or giveaways for featured pets, the salon not only showcases its grooming services but also builds a sense of community among pet owners.

By addressing the big question of *"how do I get*

more followers?" and implementing strategic tactics with engaging examples to attract and retain followers, you can create a vibrant and engaged community that supports and advocates for your brand during the summer season and beyond.

CHAPTER 7: PUTTING IT ALL TOGETHER: YOUR SUMMER MARKETING CAMPAIGN

Planning Your Campaign Timeline

☐ **Starting Point:** Begin planning your summer campaign at least 2-3 months in advance. For a campaign starting at the end of June, start your preparations by early April.

☐ **Content Calendar:** Develop a detailed content calendar outlining key dates, holidays, and promotional periods. Schedule posts, videos, contests, and other engagement activities.

☐ **Setting Up Your Social Media Calendar**
  . **Frequency:** Decide how often you'll post on each

platform. Consistency is key.

- **Themes:** Assign themes to different weeks or months (e.g., "Summer Fun," "Healthy Living," "Home Improvement").
- **Integration:** Coordinate your social media efforts with other marketing channels like email newsletters, blog posts, and in-store promotions.

Crafting A Comprehensive Marketing Campaign

Crafting a comprehensive marketing campaign involves more than just planning posts and promotions; it requires a strategic approach to engage your audience and drive desired outcomes. As you develop your campaign, it's essential to consider various elements that contribute to its success, including lead magnets, tripwires, core offers, statements of value, before-and-after grids, and customer avatars.

A lead magnet serves as a valuable incentive to attract potential customers and capture their contact information. It can be a free resource, such as an eBook, checklist, webinar, or consultation, offered in exchange for an email address. For instance, the ice cream shop offers a free downloadable recipe booklet of unique ice cream flavors as a lead magnet to entice ice cream enthusiasts and build their email list.

Once you've captured leads, it's crucial to convert them into paying customers. A tripwire is a low-cost or entry-level offer designed to encourage prospects to make their first purchase. Examples include discounted services, trial memberships, or introductory courses. For instance, the plumber offers a low-cost inspection or initial service visit as a tripwire to encourage homeowners to experience their services firsthand and build trust.

Your core offer represents the main product or service you sell to your customers. It addresses their core needs or desires and represents the highest value and revenue potential for your business. Examples include service packages, subscription plans, or flagship products. For example, the realtor offers real estate buying/ selling service packages as their core offer, providing comprehensive solutions to clients looking for their dream homes.

Your statement of value communicates the unique benefits and value proposition of your product or service to potential customers. It highlights what sets your offering apart from competitors and why customers should choose it. A compelling statement of value helps differentiate your business and attract the attention of your target audience. For instance, the nutritionist's statement of value, *"Achieve your healthiest summer yet with personalized guidance,"* emphasizes the unique value proposition of their coaching program and appeals to individuals seeking to improve their health and wellness.

Examples:

Ice Cream Shop

Theme:	"Cool Treats for Hot Days"
Hashtags:	#SummerScoop, #CoolTreats
Promotion:	Weekly flavor highlights, customer photo contests, summer loyalty programs.

Engagement:	Host an "Ice Cream Day" event with live music and free samples.
Lead Magnet:	Free downloadable recipe booklet of unique ice cream flavors.
Tripwire:	Offer a discounted first scoop or small cone for new customers.
Core Offer:	Seasonal ice cream subscription or loyalty program.
Statement of Value:	"Experience the coolest treats this summer, handcrafted with love."
Profit Maximizer:	Upsell larger sizes or add toppings and premium flavors.
Return Path:	Collect customer emails for monthly newsletters with exclusive offers.

Realtor

Theme:	"Finding Your Summer Dream Home"
Hashtags	#SummerHomes, #DreamHomeHunt
Promotion:	Virtual home tours, tips for buying/selling in summer, client success stories.
Engagement:	Run a referral program and host neighborhood open house events.
Lead Magnet:	Free eBook on "Top 10 Tips for Buying a Home in the Summer."

Tripwire:	Offer a free consultation or home valuation.
Core Offer:	Real estate buying/selling service packages.
Statement of Value:	"Helping you find the perfect home to enjoy your summer."
Profit Maximizer:	Partner with local moving companies or interior designers for bundled services.
Return Path:	Follow up with clients for testimonials and referrals; send market updates.

Plumber

Theme:	"Keeping Your Home Summer-Ready"
Hashtags	#SummerPlumbing, #HomeMaintenance
Promotion:	Summer maintenance tips, special discounts on seasonal services.
Engagement:	Q&A sessions on common plumbing issues, tutorial videos.
Lead Magnet:	Checklist for "Summer Plumbing Maintenance Tips."
Tripwire:	Low-cost inspection or initial service visit.
Core Offer:	Comprehensive plumbing maintenance plans.
Statement of	"Ensuring your home stays cool and

Value:	leak-free all summer long."
Profit Maximizer:	Offer water-saving devices or upgrades.
Return Path:	Schedule follow-up services and send reminders for seasonal maintenance.

Nutritionist/Coach

Theme:	"Healthy Summer Living"
Hashtags	#SummerWellness, #HealthyLiving
Promotion:	Summer meal plans, fitness challenges, success stories.
Engagement:	Host weekly live sessions on nutrition and wellness tips.
Lead Magnet:	Free "7-Day Summer Detox Plan" or workout guide.
Tripwire:	Affordable introductory online consultation or mini-course.
Core Offer:	Full coaching program with personalized meal and fitness plans.
Statement of Value:	"Achieve your healthiest summer yet with personalized guidance."
Profit Maximizer:	Add one-on-one coaching sessions or premium supplements.
Return Path:	Regular check-ins and follow-up programs; newsletters with tips and success stories.

If you really want to elevate your marketing strategy, consider working with a professional marketing strategist. They can help you determine the product-market fit and complete essential tools like a before-and-after grid and a detailed customer avatar. These steps will provide deeper insights into your market and ensure your campaign is both targeted and effective.

A before-and-after grid visually showcases the transformation or results achieved by using your product or service. It features side-by-side comparisons of the "before" state (the customer's problem or pain point) and the "after" state (the solution provided by your offering). This grid helps potential customers visualize the benefits and outcomes of using your offering, making it more compelling and persuasive.

Developing a detailed customer avatar, or buyer persona, helps you better understand your target audience's needs, preferences, and behaviors. It includes demographic information, interests, pain points, goals, and motivations, enabling you to create more targeted and effective marketing campaigns. By understanding your customers better, you can tailor your messaging and offerings to resonate with their specific needs and preferences.

By incorporating all of the above elements into your marketing campaign, you can create a comprehensive and effective strategy tailored to your business needs. From attracting leads with compelling lead magnets to converting them into paying customers with enticing tripwires, and delivering value with your core offer and statement of value, each element plays a crucial role in driving the success of your campaign. Additionally, leveraging before-and-after grids and customer avatars provides deeper insights into your target audience and helps you create more targeted and impactful marketing messages.

Monitoring and adjusting your campaign is also crucial for its success. Regularly check the performance of your posts and promotions using tools like Google Analytics, social media insights, and feedback forms. Be prepared to adjust your strategy based on what's working and what's not, staying responsive to trends and audience feedback. This flexibility allows you to optimize your efforts and ensure your campaign remains effective and engaging.

By following these guidelines and utilizing these marketing elements, you can create a comprehensive and effective summer marketing campaign tailored to your business needs. This approach ensures that you start strong, stay consistent, and achieve your seasonal business goals.

Don't Fret: It's Never Too Late To Start

If you're just reading this now and need to come up with a campaign quickly, don't worry! It's never too late to boost your business this summer. Follow the steps outlined in this eBook, and you can still create an effective and engaging marketing campaign. Start by setting clear goals, developing a concise plan, and leveraging the tips and strategies provided. With a focused approach, you can make a significant impact, even with a short lead time. Let's get started and make this summer a success for your business!

CHAPTER 8: UNDERSTANDING ORGANIC SOCIAL MEDIA VS. PAID ADVERTISING

Throughout this book, we have focused primarily on leveraging organic social media to build and engage your audience. Now, let's explore the differences between organic social media and paid advertising, particularly how paid advertising works, the rules, and the costs associated with various platforms such as Facebook, Instagram, LinkedIn, Twitter, TikTok, and Google My Business (GMB). We'll also provide examples for different types of businesses, including an ice cream shop, realtor, plumber, medi-spa, and nutritionist.

Organic Social Media

Organic social media involves using free tools provided by social media platforms to grow and engage with an audience. The benefits include building a loyal community, fostering long-term engagement, and creating authentic connections with followers. Strategies to grow organic reach include consistently creating high-quality content, engaging actively with your audience, and building a community around your brand.

Here are some examples we have previously explored:
- **Ice cream shop:** post daily photos of their new flavors, host live tastings on Instagram, and engage with customers by responding to comments and messages.
- **Realtor:** share success stories of clients finding their dream homes, provide tips for first-time buyers, and engage in local community groups to establish trust and authority.
- **Plumber:** post helpful DIY tips for minor repairs, showcasing their expertise and reliability.
- **Medi-spa:** share client testimonials and behind-the-scenes looks at their services, Nutritionist: could offer daily health tips and nutritious recipes to build credibility and rapport with their audience.
- **Nutritionist/Coach:** address popular summer wellness topics like staying fit while traveling or

navigating social gatherings with healthy eating tips and strategies to keep clients on track with their goals.

However, the limitations of organic reach have become more pronounced due to algorithm changes on platforms like Facebook and Instagram, which prioritize paid content and user connections over organic posts from businesses. Despite the engaging content, businesses might find that their posts are only reaching a fraction of their followers unless they boost visibility through paid promotions.

Paid Social Media Advertising

Paid social media advertising involves spending money to display advertisements or sponsored messages to social media users. This approach offers greater control over who sees your content and can significantly boost reach and engagement. Paid advertising includes various types, such as sponsored posts, display ads, and video ads. For instance, a plumber can use Facebook ads to target local homeowners experiencing plumbing issues, ensuring their services are seen by a relevant audience.While organic efforts build long-term engagement, paid ads can quickly drive traffic and conversions. A medi-spa might use Instagram ads to showcase before-and-after images of treatments, targeting users interested in beauty and wellness, resulting in a higher return on investment (ROI) compared to solely relying on organic reach. Similarly, a nutritionist might run targeted ads promoting a new online course, quickly attracting interested participants from a broader audience.

How Paid Advertising Works: Ad Creation And Targeting

Creating an ad campaign involves several steps. First, define your campaign objective, whether it's brand awareness, website traffic, or conversions. Then, choose your target audience based on demographics, interests, and behaviors. Custom and lookalike audiences can be particularly effective; for example, a nutritionist might target people who have previously shown interest in health and wellness products and also create a lookalike audience based on their most engaged followers.

A custom audience is a group of users that you create based on specific criteria. For example, if you're a nutritionist running an ad campaign, you might create a custom audience consisting of people who have interacted with your website, signed up for your newsletter, or engaged with your content on social media. These are individuals who have already shown some level of interest in your services or products.

A lookalike audience is a group of users who share similar characteristics, interests, and behaviors to your custom audience. In the example provided, the nutritionist creates a lookalike audience based on their most engaged followers. This means that the social media platform (e.g., Facebook) analyzes the characteristics and behaviors of the nutritionist's existing audience and then identifies other users who exhibit similar traits but may not yet be familiar with the nutritionist's services.

So, in simple terms, a lookalike audience is a way to expand your reach beyond your existing customer base by targeting new users who are likely to be interested in your products or services because they resemble your current customers in terms of their behaviors and interests. It's like finding new potential clients who have traits similar to your existing satisfied clients.

Next, select the appropriate ad format. There are various options, including image ads, video ads, carousel ads, and stories. Choosing the right format depends on your campaign goals and audience preferences. For instance, an ice cream shop might use carousel ads on Instagram to showcase multiple flavors, enticing users with visually appealing images. A realtor might use video ads to give virtual tours of properties, while a plumber could utilize short, informative videos demonstrating their services. A medi-spa might find success with Instagram Stories, providing quick glimpses of their treatments, and a nutritionist might use TikTok ads to share engaging, educational content about healthy living.

Platform-Specific Rules And Features

Different platforms have unique rules and features for paid advertising. On Facebook, the Ads Manager provides comprehensive tools for creating and managing ads. It's important to adhere to Facebook's advertising policies, which cover prohibited content and community standards. Costs on Facebook are influenced by factors such as bidding strategies and ad quality. For example, an ice cream shop might set a budget to promote a new seasonal flavor, ensuring the ad reaches local customers likely to visit the shop.

Instagram integrates with Facebook Ads Manager, making it easy to manage campaigns across both platforms. Popular ad formats on Instagram include stories and posts, and influencer partnerships can be highly effective. A medi-spa might collaborate with beauty influencers to promote their treatments through sponsored content, reaching a wider audience and adding credibility to their services.

LinkedIn offers excellent B2B targeting options, including sponsored content and InMail. This platform is ideal for targeting professional audiences, such as a realtor looking to connect with potential clients in specific industries. Costs are generally higher due to the professional nature of the audience, but the targeted reach can be highly effective.

Twitter's promoted tweets and trends help increase visibility. It's essential to use concise messaging and compelling visuals. A plumber might use promoted tweets to share emergency service promotions, targeting users in their service area with timely and relevant offers.

TikTok's short-form video ad formats are perfect for engaging younger audiences. Influencer collaborations and branded hashtags can amplify reach. A nutritionist could create engaging, educational videos on healthy eating, using TikTok ads to reach a wider audience quickly and effectively.

Google My Business (GMB) is crucial for local businesses. Local search ads can boost visibility for businesses like plumbers and ice cream shops. GMB ads are typically cost-effective and essential for driving local traffic. For example, a plumber might use GMB ads to appear at the top of local search results, ensuring they are the first option for users seeking emergency services.

Factors Influencing Cost

Paid advertising costs are influenced by various factors, including CPC (Cost Per Click), CPM (Cost Per Thousand Impressions), and CPA (Cost Per Action). Industry benchmarks and typical cost ranges vary by platform and ad type. For example, CPC for a nutritionist on Facebook might differ from CPM for a medi-spa on Instagram. A realtor might find LinkedIn ads more expensive but also more effective for reaching high-value clients.

Ad relevance and quality scores significantly affect cost. Higher relevance and quality can reduce costs and improve performance. Setting and managing budgets is crucial; businesses can choose between daily and lifetime budgets.

Allocating the budget based on campaign goals and platform performance, and continuously monitoring and adjusting budgets, ensures optimal results.

Setting And Managing Budgets

Businesses should decide between daily and lifetime budgets based on their campaign needs. For instance, an ice cream shop might set a daily budget to promote a weekly special, ensuring consistent visibility throughout the week. A realtor might opt for a lifetime budget for a property listing campaign, spreading the budget over the duration of the listing. Monitoring and adjusting budgets based on real-time performance data is essential for optimizing results and ensuring that advertising spend is used effectively.

In terms of costs, small businesses might spend around CAD $500 to $1,000 per month on Facebook and Instagram ads, while more extensive campaigns might require CAD $5,000 to $10,000 or more. LinkedIn ads tend to be more expensive, with typical budgets starting at CAD $1,000 to $2,000 per month. Twitter and TikTok ads can vary widely, but a reasonable starting budget might be CAD $500 to $2,000 per month. GMB ads are generally cost-effective, with many businesses finding success with monthly budgets as low as CAD $100 to $300.

Challenges Of Diy Advertising Vs. Using A Marketing Agency

Setting up and managing ad campaigns on platforms like Meta Business Suite (for Facebook and Instagram) and Google Ads can be challenging for those without experience. Each platform has its own interface, rules, and best practices. For example, creating effective audience segments, choosing the right bidding strategies, and designing compelling ad creatives require a good understanding of the platform and digital marketing principles.

Business owners might find it time-consuming and confusing to navigate Facebook Ads Manager and LinkedIn's targeting options leading to suboptimal ad performance. Others could find it difficult to track and optimize Google Ads campaigns effectively. The time and effort required to learn and manage these platforms can detract from running the core business.

Hiring a marketing company can alleviate these challenges. Professional marketers have the expertise and experience to create, manage, and optimize ad campaigns efficiently. They stay updated with the latest trends and changes in platform algorithms, ensuring your ads perform at their best.

That said, the cost of hiring a marketing company can be significant. Fees can range from CAD $1,000 to $3,000 per month for small to medium-sized businesses, with larger businesses potentially spending CAD $5,000 to $10,000 or more per month. Despite the higher costs, the improved ROI from professionally managed campaigns often justifies the expense. For any business looking to expand their online presence, the expertise of a marketing company can be invaluable in reaching a broader audience and driving conversions.

Examples:

- **Ice Cream Shop:** Use Facebook's Local Awareness ads to target people within a specific radius of your shop, promoting a new flavor or special event to drive local foot traffic. Create a Google Ads campaign using location-based targeting and seasonal keywords to attract customers searching for summer treats.
- **Realtor:** Utilize Facebook's Dynamic Ads for Real Estate to show personalized property listings based on users' browsing behavior, increasing the chances of attracting serious buyers. Run LinkedIn Lead Gen Form ads to capture details of potential clients interested in buying or selling properties, focusing on high-value areas and professional demographics.
- **Plumber:** Use Google Local Services ads to appear at the top of search results for emergency plumbing services, ensuring high visibility and trust with the Google Guaranteed badge. Implement retargeting ads on Facebook to reach users who visited your website but didn't book a service, offering a special discount to entice them back.
- **Medi Spa:** Partner with local beauty influencers to create sponsored content and Stories, showcasing your treatments and building credibility among their followers. Create high-quality video ads demonstrating popular treatments and client

testimonials, targeting users interested in skincare and wellness on YouTube.

- **Nutritionist/Coach:** Promote engaging and informative content through sponsored posts and Stories on Instagram, targeting users interested in health, fitness, and wellness. Run Facebook Live ads promoting free webinars or live Q&A sessions about nutrition and healthy living, encouraging sign-ups for personalized coaching sessions.

Measuring And Analyzing Performance

Key Metrics:

Key metrics to track include impressions, reach, clicks, and CTR (Click-Through Rate). Each platform offers specific metrics and KPIs, so it's important to familiarize yourself with these to gauge performance accurately. For example, a medi-spa might track the number of bookings made through a specific Instagram ad, while a plumber might measure the number of service requests generated from a Facebook campaign.

Tools and Reports:

Built-in analytics tools on each platform provide initial

insights, while third-party tools can offer deeper analysis. For instance, a nutritionist might use Facebook Insights to track engagement metrics and Google Analytics to measure website traffic from social media ads. Third-party tools can provide comprehensive cross-platform analysis, helping businesses understand their overall advertising performance and make data-driven decisions.

Optimizing Campaigns:

Optimizing campaigns involves A/B testing different ad elements to find the most effective combinations. For example, an ice cream shop might test different images and copy to see which ads drive the most foot traffic to their store. Iterative improvements based on data and performance feedback can significantly enhance campaign outcomes. A realtor might experiment with different targeting options to find the most responsive audience, while a medi-spa could test various ad formats to see which generates the most appointment bookings.

Ad Policies and Legal Considerations:

Understanding each platform's ad approval processes and common reasons for rejection helps in creating compliant ads. Legal requirements, such as GDPR and CCPA, must also be adhered to ensure data privacy and protection. For instance, a nutritionist collecting client information through ads must ensure compliance with data protection regulations to avoid legal issues.

Best Practices:

Crafting compelling ad copy and visuals is essential for capturing attention. Ads should be scheduled for peak engagement times without overwhelming the audience. Ethical considerations, such as maintaining authenticity and avoiding misleading content, are crucial for building trust. For example, a medi-spa should use real client testimonials and avoid exaggerated claims about treatment results.

By incorporating these key points, this chapter provides a comprehensive understanding of the differences between organic social media and paid advertising. Throughout this book, we've emphasized how organic social media is essential for getting businesses started and keeping them relevant through regular posting and engagement. However, the main drawback of organic social media is its limited reach due to evolving algorithms and platform policies. To overcome this challenge, integrating paid advertising can significantly enhance visibility and engagement. When done correctly, combining organic and paid strategies allows businesses like ice cream shops, realtors, plumbers, medi-spas, and nutritionists to effectively maximize their social media presence and drive better overall results.

Congratulations!

You've reached the end of **The Ultimate Summer Social Media Playbook**. Armed with the strategies and tips outlined in this guide, you're ready to take your social media presence to new heights and make this summer your most successful season yet. Remember to stay flexible, experiment with different approaches, and most importantly, have fun engaging with your audience and showcasing your brand's unique personality. Here's to a sizzling summer of social media success!

But wait, there's more!

As a **special offer** for our valued readers, we're excited to invite you to claim your **free social media marketing strategy session** tailored to your business. During this personalized session, our expert team will dive deep into your social media goals, challenges, and opportunities, and provide you with actionable insights and recommendations to elevate your summer social media strategy. Whether you're looking to boost engagement, increase visibility, or drive conversions, we're here to help you achieve your goals!

EMPOWER YOUR BUSINESS

"I want to assure you that your success is our top priority. With over 15 years of experience in sales, management, and leadership roles, I've honed my skills in driving revenue, optimizing operations, and enhancing brand visibility. Additionally, our partnership with Blam Partners ensures that your digital needs are met with expertise, professionalism and excellence. "

Free Digital Marketing Strategy Consultation

Craft a comprehensive plan to optimize your online presence, targeting your audience effectively.

Schedule your Free Strategy Session Now

Learn more about our Social Media Packages

www.vitalixdigital.ca